# Profit 911

## A Real-World Guide To Getting More Customers And Putting More Cash In Your Pocket While Working Less And Reducing Stress

**Justin Miller**

# DEDICATION

This book is dedicated to all my business friends and associates that have pushed me to help others with my business and marketing knowledge. It has been a very rewarding journey doing so and I hope to continue helping other businesses for as long as possible.

# Table of Contents

# ACKNOWLEDGMENTS

This book would not be possible without contributions from several people. I want to take a moment to thank just a few of them. Special thanks to Happy Joe Whitty, Joe Slavens, and Jim Russell for sitting down with me for interviews to contribute to this book. Also thanks to some of my marketing mentors over the years including, but not limited to: Dave Dee, Dan Kennedy, Michael Gerber, Bradley Sugars, Dave Ramsey, Geoff Ronning, Tim Ferriss, and countless others. It is their teachings that have allowed me to do what I love and to help others do the same.

# 1. Introduction

Congratulations! I say congratulations because you've just taken the first step in making your business even more successful. You see, most people get stuck working IN their businesses and never take the time to work ON the business. They refuse to invest a few hours to read a book that will provide them the equivalent of years of experience struggling on their own. This is often a fatal flaw. By the sheer fact that you picked up this book and are reading it, I know that you are among the few who are destined to succeed. Getting the knowledge is one thing but you also need to make sure you actually take the time to act on what you learn.

I want you to promise yourself right now that you will begin to change. You will take your business more seriously and work on what matters. You are ready to make big changes for big results. You know that if you keep doing the same thing over and over, things won't change and eventually your business will fail. This book is a new beginning and starting point for you.

A few words about the content of this book before we begin. As you read, you will find two different types of information in this book. You'll find strategy as well as actual tactics. Both types of information will serve you well. However, most people have a tendency to look towards the tactics without understanding the actual strategies behind them. In order to be effective in business, you need to understand both the strategy, as well as the tactics used to accomplish that strategy.

This book is intended to be read by and be useful to small business owners that are actually operating businesses with their own blood, sweat, tears, and money at stake. While this book can also serve a new business launch well, it does not lay out the starting mechanics of a business. I am going to assume that you already have a business that is generating revenue and you are seeking to take that business to the next level. I am also going to assume that you provide a good quality service to your customer. If not, implementing the ideas in this book will actually accelerate the failure of your business. With that in mind, let's proceed.

As you read, try not to get overwhelmed with the amount of ideas in this book. I have given you 90% of the tactics we use in a business that has been operating over 15 years. They were not all implemented at the same time or overnight; but the quicker you can put things into place, the better your results will be. As you read, try to think of what you can put in place immediately and what you think will work best for your business. Put a post-it note on those pages or get out a notebook and take notes as you read. I tried really hard to not hold back anything in this book, but the downside to doing so is the possibility of overwhelming you.

I suggest you take a few ideas at a time from this book and then revisit it again once those are in place.

In the back of this book you will find a resource directory with many of the products and service providers we use to operate our business. These resources are constantly changing as technology evolves, so they may or may not be up-to-date. For this reason, you will also find our up-to-date list of resources on our website. See the resources section of this book for additional details on how to access our up-to-date "Million Dollar Resource Directory".

# 2. How This Book Will Change Your Life

Depending upon how you heard about this book, you may be wondering who on earth Justin Miller is and why should I listen to him. While this book is not a biography on my life or business dealings, it's useful to understand my background and where I come from. I will share several personal examples from my business throughout the text here.

Ever since I can remember, I've always been thinking of ways to make money. When I was in grade school, you would often find me walking around the neighborhood door-to-door selling greeting cards, Boy Scout popcorn, collecting cans, and doing just about anything else to make a buck. In fact, I think it was about the age of 12 that I hired my first "employee" to help me sell buttons and magnets in my button making business. His name was Nick and he lived two blocks from my parents' house. I have always been the type to find a way to go out and do something rather than complain about my circumstances. If your story sounds similar, then I have no doubt you are already on the right path. Business is all about finding ways to make the impossible happen. If it was easy, everyone would do it. It is also important to realize that *ALL* successful businesspeople have also had their fair share of failures. Often, the failures outweigh the successes quite heavily, but it only takes one good success to have it made for the rest of your life.

At the age of about 14, I started my current business called Master Entertainment. This company primarily provided disc jockeys for schools, parties, and weddings in Illinois and Iowa. Over the years, we expanded our services to include a variety of other things such as live trivia game shows, outdoor inflatable movie screens, comedy stage hypnosis, and countless others. It currently employs a staff of about 12 people from our office in Moline, Illinois. At this point, I only work in this business on Mondays and my staff does the rest and handles most of the day-to-day operations.

Master Entertainment has been operated by me from my parent's house, in a dorm room at Northern Illinois University, in an apartment, from my home, and now from a professional office space. I ran the business while simultaneously getting a bachelor's degree in business management as well as a master's degree in business administration.

Over the years, I have invested and reinvested well over $1 million into this business and have had many failures and successes along the way. The one constant thing throughout all this was my love for marketing. You see, it was not the business that I was in that was the fun part. It was finding out how to get customers, how to sell to those customers, and how to maximize revenue from those customers.

Any time we had a new product or service, it was a new adventure and a new challenge to figure out how to get into the marketplace and how to make profit as quickly as possible. Every time we've done this, we have gotten better and better and learned more and more. Our most recent launch (a photo booth business) actually paid off our initial investment with cash in bank within a week (with zero cash investment on our part) and did well over $100,000 its first year. In fact, we have gotten to the point with our core disc jockey business where we have 85% market share of our target audience. This is relatively unheard of in any industry and were it a larger industry, would be considered a monopoly.

With the business at 85% market share, I decided it was time for me to personally do something else. I promoted a staff member to general manager from within the company and am focusing my time on helping other small businesses. For years and years, many of my other friends who own businesses came to me for marketing advice. They would literally call me for hours at a time asking me to help them with their businesses and to bounce ideas off of me. While I was operating the Master Entertainment business, I did not have the time to help them. Now that I've switched gears, this book you are reading is the start of that business. I am not holding anything back in this book other than that due to page limitations. I will share many strategies with you that cost me tens of thousands of dollars to learn as well as proven tactics that have yielded hundreds of thousands of dollars of sales year after year.

I speak from my own personal experiences running my own business, not just consulting fluff from someone that has never had to meet payroll. In addition, I do have a master's degree in business so I have seen that side of business as well. I am bringing a lot to the table for you to help you succeed.

# 3. The Problems of Small Business Owners

There are many problems with running small businesses that owners encounter over and over again. Often times, they were able to build their business through friends and family and in an environment with little competition. As time went on, the world got smaller and smaller through the use of the Internet and technology. The game of business has changed drastically and many people are now playing catch-up trying to protect what they worked so hard for. They also run into problems with needing more and more sales and cash to make their business worthwhile each and every year as expenses continue to escalate as the business grows.

Without even looking at the big picture, you may have seen these changes coming. But what usually happens is you are so focused and so busy on actually delivering your product or service that by the time you see the train coming down the tracks, it has already run over you. All of a sudden you look up and realize that all the money you worked so hard for has disappeared from the business bank account, leaving you with poverty wages.

Most entrepreneurs are not afraid of work, and that's the good news. The problem is that most people are focusing their efforts and their work in the wrong areas. They think that if they just had more hours in the day than they could make a lot more money. That philosophy is just wrong – and that is actually a good thing once you realize it. Everybody has an equal playing field as far as how many hours are in a day. It's what you do with them that makes the difference. Knowing what to do with those hours is one thing I'm going to help you with. It is often said that if you are self employed, you can work whatever 80 hours per week you want. The outside world has no idea what it takes to be a business owner. You do the impossible every day and work for the world's most difficult boss, yourself.

If you have grown to the point where you have employees, you probably have a whole different set of problems. Every time you turn your back, a staff member screws something up. They just can't do anything without asking about it. It's so bad that often times you just end up doing it yourself to save the hassle of someone bringing you the poor work after interrupting you 20 times with questions about how to do something. You are working seven days a week, 12 hours a day, and just not seeing the money at the end of the month that you could be making as an employee of another company putting in those kind of hours. You started your own business for freedom and now it's consuming your whole life. You have become a prisoner to your business. You do everything from business strategy to cleaning the toilets. You don't feel you can hire additional qualified staff because there is just not money to do so. I get it. I've been there. It's common. You are not alone.

The best part is that there are solutions to all of these problems. Even better is that working harder is not necessarily the solution. Often times, the fewer hours I work the more dollars that come in the door. That can't happen if the groundwork is not laid and you're not focusing your time in the right areas. When I work with consulting clients, I often ask them to write what percentage of their day they think is productive. I will oftentimes see responses of 10% to 20%. That means if I can just help them to get to say 70% or 80% productive, then they should see triple or quadruple the results. It's all about clearing out the distractions and the miscellaneous tasks that can be done elsewhere. But in order to do so, you need to know how to manage the staff and the technology that can make that happen for you.

Here is what one of my consulting clients had to say about his staff, "Everybody asks me everything. Every little thing, *EVERY LITTLE THING.* They will walk up in the office just to tell me, 'You know, a tree fell down in the woods.' Are you kidding me? You walked all the way from point A, thirty acres out there, to the building to tell me a tree fell?" The sad part is that he is not alone and that it is partly his behavior that causes the staff to think it is acceptable to act like this.

How do you solve a problem like this? Well there a couple different ways, but they both involve isolating yourself from the other staff members. I know you may be thinking that's impossible to do. You have to work with them to get the job done. To a certain extent you're right, but this doesn't have to be the case all the time. You can put physical barriers such as closed-door hours and do not disturb signs. You can shut your phone off or you can train them to not interrupt you. At some point, you will even want to make sure you put a staff member between you and the rest of your staff so you only have one person to train. If you were President of the United States that would be the Chief of Staff's job.

As Dave Ramsey likes to say in his *'Entreleadership'* teachings, When an employee walks into the office with a problem it's like they have a monkey on their back. That monkey is the problem and it is your job to make sure that when they walk out that door they take their monkey back with them. Otherwise, pretty soon your office will turn into a zoo with all the monkeys running loose.

I know that when the business is struggling or not moving as quickly you want it to it's very difficult. It's rough mentally. It's draining every day going into work. The good news is that once things start moving in the right direction, your mentality quickly becomes positive. It becomes fun again. Sometimes it takes a little time away to get there mentally. But once you're moving in the right direction, it is a massive relief. There are plenty of tactics in this book to turn you on the right path and get your passion and drive back.

Once you become more successful, you will start to encounter an entirely different set of problems. You may outgrow your current staff's skills. You will have tons of opportunities trying to shift your attention into new areas that may or may not yield results. Cash flow can become very difficult in a successful growing company. In fact, it is often said that the biggest problem with a million dollar business is that it costs a million dollars to operate. I agree with this wholeheartedly, but once again you wouldn't be the first person encountering these problems and they can be overcome. It is up to you to seek out solutions and ways to overcome these problems. Don't just give up. Go for it!

# 4. The 15 Year Overnight Success

So you have built your business to some arbitrary level of *'success'*, now what? You will soon learn that everybody wants a piece of your success and nobody gives you credit for your work and knowledge that made it happen. You will often be considered an overnight success when in reality, you had been preparing for that metaphorical night for a decade.

In my life, that was with the launch of our photo booth rental business. $100,000 of highly profitable revenue within 12 months. Most outsiders would consider that lucky. They wouldn't see that I spent ten years learning piece by piece what to do when "opportunity came knocking." They didn't see the 2-3 years of research specific to this launch. This is why they will never be able to replicate the results.

You need to arm yourself with all the knowledge, tools, and abilities to be able to strike when the iron is hot. That time may be right now for you. It may be coming up. Don't let it catch you off guard. Opportunities are rarely repeated and don't wait for you to catch-up to them. They are speeding aircrafts and if you miss the take-off then you are left with scraps of what could have been. You will sit around and say I had that idea and that somebody else stole it from you. Don't think of what riches you could have. Prepare and act when opportunity arises. Take decisive action.

# 5. You Can't Do It Alone

After all the problems with staff, why not just work alone? Surely it can be done easier by yourself, right? You can to a certain extent but it will greatly limit your earning potential. Often times, small-business owners are able to build a business to $200,000 or $300,000 in revenue through primarily their own efforts and hard work. If you want to go beyond that, or you want there to be more profit, or you want to build your company to where you actually own a business instead of working within your business, then you need to have a different game plan. Take some things off your plate and put them on some others. Eliminate unnecessary tasks.

At some point, you need to look into the idea of what it's costing you to do all the small tasks as opposed to paying someone else to do them. You need to focus on your most profitable core activities. That often times (if not all the time) is the sales and marketing tasks. An hour spent in sales and marketing can often yield hundreds, if not thousands of dollars in results. Whereas, an hour spent sorting papers can be hired out for $10 an hour and yields no revenue regardless of who does it. When you begin to understand that the $10 is what is holding you back, your course of action day-to-day will change drastically. You need to find a balance between hard work and your money working for you.

# 6. High Performance Staff

If you are reading this book in search of answers on how to grow your business, then you are probably at a point where you have to get some help in your business. This is the only way to clear up some time for important tasks. If you have more free time than money, then you will still be the one doing the work. At the same time, you will be laying the foundation for the point when the duties are transitioned to somebody else. That is what is going to have to happen. Regardless of whether it is you or someone else, someone has got to start taking some tasks off your plate so you can focus your efforts on what you are most skilled at and will yield the best results. For instance, if you are a homebuilder, then you should not be making deliveries to job sites. If you are a dentist, you should not be sorting patient files at the end of the day or cleaning the bathrooms. If you are a chiropractor, you shouldn't be spending valuable time sorting incoming mail.

If you do too much stuff on your own for too long, you will begin to feel burnout and start to hate the job you used to love. To prevent this, it is important to take time to disconnect. With a constant connection to the Internet via our cell phones and gadgets, unless you make a conscious effort to disconnect, it will not happen. When you do not disconnect, rest assured that you will feel stressed.

Here's a personal example from my own business. I used to have my cell phone on me 24 hours a day, 7 days a week with the ringer always turned on. It was in my pocket during the day and it was on the nightstand when I went to bed. I would get text messages and calls at all hours from staff for a variety of different reasons. Rarely were any of these reasons what I would consider to be an emergency. In fact, most of our business fulfillment is conducted on Saturday evenings.

If you were paying attention earlier, then you probably noted that at this point, I only work in that business on Mondays. This means that I am not going to be the one that the staff is calling on Saturday to help them with their minor problems while doing their jobs. I have a 24-hour answering service that takes calls and will route messages to other staff members, should they need it. The service is actually surprisingly cheap. If you want more information on what company we use, please see the resource directory in the back of this book.

On most nights, my phone is either turned completely off or is in a different room in the house where I will not be disturbed by it. Every once in a while, something legitimately goes wrong in the business operations. In fact, it will sometimes cost me money to rectify the situation when Monday rolls around. That being said, it is well worth the small expense in order to have my freedom back and de-stress when not at work. On top of that, the staff does surprisingly well handling situations on their own when they know they can't reach me and must resolve things on their own or wait for my assistance.

# 7. Business Systems & Processes

Let's start with getting a common misunderstanding out of the way. Your staff is never going to "get it." They didn't start the business. They haven't had the experience you did before the business. So you have to give them exact processes. The only thing you can really criticize them for is if they don't follow an exact process. If you give them what they need to succeed, you will be pleasantly surprised. If you don't, they will likely fail and you will blame them for not being able to do the job, but it is really your own fault. They are employees, not entrepreneurs or business owners. They can be taught to make decisions like you would, but they need to know the criteria you use when making a decision.

So right now, your business probably isn't set up to where you have all those processes available. That's okay, but it is one thing you have got to work on. You need to get the processes laid out to where people know what to expect and that way they can get it done. And yes, it's a constant battle. While in theory, you believe that you can setup the systems once and they work perfect forever, reality is different. In reality, things change and people come and go. But overall, an hour spent implementing systems may yield hundreds of hours of someone else working instead of you doing it all. If your company gets big enough, you can even document a training system and have a staff member  train your system to new employees.

The biggest thing that holds back businesses is the business owner getting in the way of himself or herself. In fact, if you are successful, your business can and likely will outgrow your skills. You either adapt and learn new skills or keep doing the same thing. Eventually your competitor is going to catch up.

Let's talk about the thought most business owners have: "I can deal with it better than anyone else."

Let's just accept it as a truth for the sake of argument, okay (even though I don't think it usually is)? At one point or another, every other business owner feels this way, including myself. Regardless of how qualified someone who comes in is, you are going to see it and think that your way is better. It may or may not be but that is actually irrelevant to the discussion.

What you have to figure out is what is the *'good enough'* level for any given job task. Now, you don't necessarily want to specify to that staff member the minimum good enough. You want to push them. Within your head, you need to know what that acceptable level is. You do need to express to the staff member what is expected of them (even if your minimum acceptable level is even lower). From that point, you need to setup the staff for success, get out of the way, and even allow them to make non-catastrophic failures. Once that is done, you can actually become a manager instead of a front-line worker. You will need to now focus on managing your systems and making sure your methods are being followed.

For more on this topic read Michael E Gerber's Book "The E-Myth".

# 8. Marketing Magnetism

Why is marketing important and such a strong focus of time for me and other business owners? The fact is, if you can market as well as we do, then you can get premium prices for your services, easier clients to work with, and more profit in your bank account when it's all said and done. Clients will come banging on your door with wallets in-hand rather than you having to chase them down. When clients come to you, you have the power in the business relationship and will reap the financial rewards. The goal of successful marketing campaigns is to make that happen. To magnetically attract customers best-suited to do business with you and spend the highest amount of money.

In my entertainment company, our services are priced anywhere from 2 to 8 times that of our competitors. Proper marketing is the only way I can get the rates I do for these services. Did you notice I did NOT say you have to have THE BEST at what you do in order to get the highest rates? Once again, I am assuming you are a rock-star at what you do, but being the best doesn't do much for you if nobody else knows it but you. It is often the smartest marketers that run the best businesses (and can actually then employ or buy out companies that are good at providing the actual product or services).

I do so much marketing that by the time a customer calls our office, or comes in for an appointment they are around 80% ready to book us. As long as I don't say anything to piss them off, we've got the business. Good marketing is what does this for you and good sales is what allows you to actually close the deal and get them to cut the check.

Another good thing about marketing is that it works at all hours for you regardless of what you are doing. If you end up in the hospital and you are the only one doing sales, you're going to see it kill your bank account right away. Your company will be right there in the hospital fighting for survival with you. If you have marketing systems in place, your staff should be able to pick up the slack if something happens to you or heaven-forbid you just want to take a vacation and shut your cell phone off. Good marketing is not guesswork. It is carefully planned, executed, and tracked. It is scientific and repeatable.

# 9. The Sales Funnel

## *The Sales Funnel*

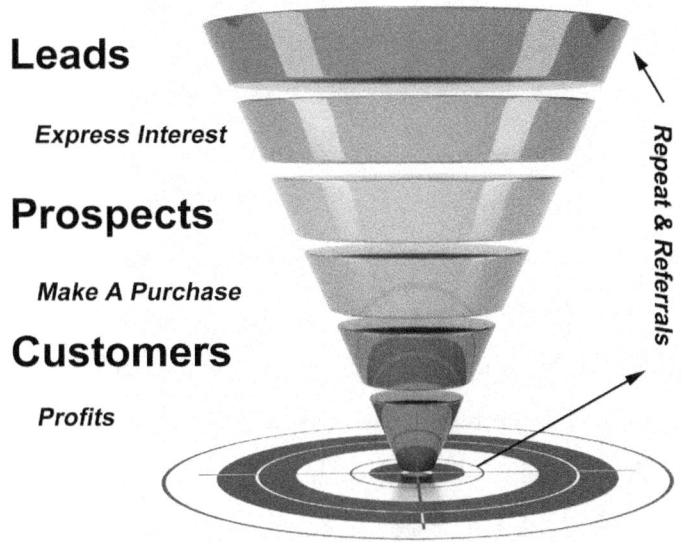

**Leads**

*Express Interest*

**Prospects**

*Make A Purchase*

**Customers**

*Profits*

*Repeat & Referrals*

The entire sales and marketing process from start to finish is represented in the above "sales funnel" diagram. The purpose of marketing is to generate leads which go into the top of the funnel. Once a lead expresses interest in something you offer (requests more info, sets up a consultation, visits the store) they become a prospect. Once a prospect actually makes a purchase they become a customer. At each step, people are lost out of the funne. That's why it gets smaller and smaller. The lower down somebody gets on the diagram, the more valuable they are to you.

Obviously the diagram is a bit of a simplification but it is valid. All you really need to do is:

1.  Get more leads in the funnel
2.  Convert a larger percentage into prospects
3.  Convert a larger percentage into customers
4.  Have each customer spend more
5.  Have each customer buy more often (repeat business)
6.  Have each customer refer more leads to you

This may seem very simple but don't underestimate the power. If we look at the following example where we have 100 leads, 50% become prospects, 50% of prospects become customers, they spend on average $500 twice per year, and one if four people refer a new customer; then we will get $31,250 in revenue. Pretty simple.

Take a look at the second column. If we do an improvement of only 10% at each level, the numbers will compound and our bottom line will be just shy of $60,000. Almost DOUBLE what we started with.

|  | Current | Plus 10% |
|---|---|---|
| **Leads** | 100 | 110 |
| **Prospects** | 50 | 66 |
| **Customers** | 25 | 39.6 |
| **Avg Purchase** | $500 | $550 |
| **Per Year** | 2 | 2.2 |
| **#Referrals** | 0.25 | 0.3 |

**$31,250**     **$59,895**

It is crucially important you understand this process and manage it in your business. It is the difference between wild success and bankruptcy. Small changes yield massive results. I encourage you to take a moment to plug your numbers in here and see what a difference can be made with a 5% or 10% improvement.

*Justin Miller*

|  | Current | Plus 10% |
|---|---|---|
| Leads |  |  |
| Prospects |  |  |
| Customers |  |  |
| Avg Purchase |  |  |
| Per Year |  |  |
| # Referrals |  |  |
|  |  |  |

# 10. Unique Selling Proposition

One concept you must master in your business is that of the unique selling proposition, or USP for short. Your USP is basically your statement of what makes you different from every other competitor. It answers the question of why should I (your potential customer) choose to do business with your company rather than any other choice including not doing business with anybody.

In order to create a USP for your company you need a very clear picture of who your target customer is and what they want. You also need a very good definition of what your company is better than everybody else at that is of value to your customer.

The classic example is Domino's old guarantee: Hot Fresh Pizza Delivered in 30 Minutes or Less or It's Free! A very powerful USP. It doesn't state the pizza is any good. It may taste like cardboard but you will get it FAST. That was important to their customers.

Little Caesar's seems to have a similar unspoken USP that you don't need to wait for pizza. It will be Hot and Ready here waiting for you. Once again, not the best pizza but no waiting. It is also cheap. They know what their customers value.

What do your target customers want? What can you

offer them that is different than anybody else and serves what they really want? This will be the basis for much of your advertising.

# 11. Customer Needs vs Wants

As a wise business owner, you must also be able to distinguish between what your customer wants and what they really need. Everybody purchases based on emotional wants on some level. We are not as rational as we would like to think when it comes to making decisions.

Here is a very advanced level sales strategy. You have to sell them what they want but deliver to them what they need. Read that again, it is very important.

If you try to sell them what they need, they probably won't buy. If you sell them what they want and only deliver what they stated they want, then they probably won't be happy campers or at a minimum, they won't become repeat customers and send you referrals. Always sell they based on what they want and in the delivery of your product or service include what they actually need. This page alone is a million dollar tip.

# 12. Why They Really Buy

Often times, what you think a client is looking for and what they are really thinking are completely different. Sometimes even the reason they tell you versus what psychologically triggers them to buy is quite different.

For example, when we provide corporate event entertainment, what we've learned is that the person we're calling on the phone when they're looking for entertainment is not actually looking for the best entertainment at all. At the same time, they're not looking for the cheapest. They're looking for the guy that won't make them look like an idiot for hiring them. All they're deeply worried about is keeping their job. If you went one step further, they want a pat on the back from their co-workers, or a thank you for hiring a person. But they definitely weren't looking for the best show.

Knowing this allowed me to present myself as the most expensive show but the safest option for them. You can use some of this philosophy against your unknowing competitors. No matter what industry you're in, I guarantee the phone callers will ask for a price? They are not actually asking the most important questions because it is subconscious. Use this to your advantage.

# 13. Testimonials & Social Proof In Advertising

One absolute truth in life and advertising is that what other people say about your business is infinitely more important that what you say about you personally. People trust other customers. They perceive you as a salesperson if you have to push them into booking.

If you were to walk into my sales office for Master Entertainment, you would be asked to have a seat in the lobby. While you are there, you are surrounded by social proof including:

- A 3-ring binder with approximately 250-300 pages of glowing customer reviews and testimonials
- A flat screen TV on the wall playing a loop of several of my TV appearances on local and regional TV shows.
- A framed poster with pictures of several dozen smiling customers
- 5 or 6 Framed thank you cards
- Chamber of commerce plaques
- A display case with copies of all the books I have written and DVDs I have produced

- A hallway lined with framed customer reviews and testimonials on the way to our conference room

By the time you are invited to meet with us in our conference room, there should be absolutely no doubt that we are the real deal and know what we are talking about. We are the trusted company by hundreds of other couples including broadcast media. This is what I mean by social proof.

What can you do in your business to increase the level of social proof?

# 14. Make It Easy For Them To Buy

When it comes time for the customer to actually make a transactional purchase and money to change hands, you need to make this as simple as possible. Once the decision to buy is made, all you can do is screw it up if you are not careful. There are several common techniques to assist you in this process.

## *Packages & Bundles:*

Create packages of commonly purchased items. Ideally you should have 3 or 4 packages. Do not give your prospect infinite choices (even if you offer them). Instead, narrow it down for them and offer them your prescription. Then shut up and let them decide.

When you have four packages (which is what I recommend) there are people that are going to take the cheapest and the most expensive, and you have to be careful that you can identify each person fairly quickly before you try and sell them package 3, or you're leaving money on the table. Package 3 should be your package you want to sell the most and most people will pick one of the middle packages and lean towards the more expensive of the two. My business is 75% on that third package to give you an example of the power of this.

You need to name your packages and present them by name – we have used gold, silver, bronze or diamond, emerald, ruby… you name it and we have tried it.

Also make sure you let them know what the most popular package is (package 3). Rest assured, they actually are booking that package more often than not. Sometimes, it's just because we told people it was the most popular. So with our pricing, it's laid out and it says 'most popular' because I don't know how many people come in my office and say, "Well, what do most people do?"

I tell them what I WANT most people to do and they do it. As long as there's value between and they are getting something more for their money on that package than they would the other ones. It becomes a self-fulfilling prophecy if presented correctly.

As an example, if the packages are $1295, $1695, $1995 and $3900. The top package are the ones that just want the best. However, I have to be really careful that if someone's looking at these, I can tell them exactly what the difference is and why it's worth enough to move up.

If they are looking at the cheapest package it's usually because they, legitimately, don't have a ton of money. They come meet with me and we just walk them up, one-by-one, like, well, in this package, you said you were interested in this.

You get this, this, and this. It normally costs $600 more but in the package, it's $400. Okay. For $300 bucks more, I'm

**42**

getting at least $600 more worth of services. All of a sudden, that's really $700 bucks on the bottom line. That's significant.

When presenting, put the most expensive on the left. Also I did some subconscious things. The cheapest one is in red. No one likes red. It's beware, danger. This "most popular" one's in green and a larger font size. Green is an action color. It means go!

## Credit Cards & Payment Plans

In today's world it is vitally important that you accept credit cards and it is so easy to do so there is no reason to not take them.

A Dunn & Bradstreet study found that people spend 12-18% more when using credit cards than when using cash. And McDonald's found that the average transaction rose from $4.50 to $7.00 when customers used plastic instead of cash. When we spend with plastic, we do not feel the same emotion as when we spend cash. It is fake money. It is easier to close sales using credit. Impulse buying is easier. It does cost you a few percent of the transaction to accept the credit card, but the increased spending easily offsets this.

There are a lot of crooks in the credit card processing industry. For a list of providers we trust, see the resource directory at the back of this book.

Also, if you set up your merchant account properly, you will be able to accept payment plans from your customers. If payment plans are not normal in your industry, I urge you to find a way to make it work for you. We can attribute over $100,000 in business won because we offered monthly payment plans and no other competitor did.

# 15. The Best Time To Sell Something

I am often asked when the best time to ask for a sale is. Well, it turns out there is one moment in time that is the easiest time to get more money out of a client. The moment is literally right after they say yes to one purchase and give you money. For this reason, you must always have another product or service to offer; or at the minimum, a deluxe version of what you just sold. Furthermore, you must ask right at that moment.

There are some very powerful psychological reasons why people are predisposed to buy again at this point, but we don't need to go into why this works in order to implement it. Start thinking right now, "What can I offer after somebody buys from me?" It even works better if you make them a one-time offer that is only valid on the spot. You don't need to be forceful or in their face. Just present the offer and let them decide.

# 16. Lead Generation

Now let's talk about what is called "lead generation advertising." The sole purpose of a lead generation ad is to get the prospect to take some sort of action to show that they are interested in wanting to learn more. You are not trying to actually sell them anything at this point, just get them to identify themselves as interested in what you have to offer.

For example, we send out postcards to companies that invite them to call or go online to get a free report on how to plan their holiday parties. When they do so, we can not only provide that report but also information about the services we offer for holiday parties. The lead has just identified themselves as interested in holiday parties so we now know that they are likely prospects for holiday party services.

Contrast this method with if we were to send a postcard saying hire us for $1,500 for your holiday party. How many responses do you think we would get? Lead generation is much more powerful and effective.

## *Lead Generation Magnets:*

You may have picked up on the fact that we offer the lead something of value to respond that we give away for free. That's called a *lead generation magnet*. What's the thing they're going to come looking for and ask for and that you can give away for free?

The best thing is usually a book of some sorts, even if it's a short book. And even if you have to pay someone to ghost write the book for you. I have authored several books for this very reason. If you're the author of a book on a certain subject, now you're the expert and you have some creditability when they call and talk to you. Even if they don't read the book, just knowing it's there has a huge impact of how you are perceived.

Here is a very advanced tip. I don't write the books to sell books. I sell a few on Amazon and our websites, but that's not the point. I give away hundreds more than I sell. I *DO NOT* make money by writing books (including this one you are reading). The reason that I write the book is it got me *TV* publicity for free on some of the stations. It got me write-ups in some of the magazines that I was able to copy and say, as seen in XYZ magazine. More importantly, everyone sees the book and is like, *Holy crap! This guy wrote a book. He must really know what he is talking about.* Well the honest truth is anyone can write a book and anyone can self-publish a book.

If you actually read some of my books, here's the real cool part. It's a 200 page sales pitch. A lot of the book was written by recording our sales pitches. I recorded it and had someone transcribe it. I edited it to where it read more like a book than a sales pitch and that's what it is. So if anyone has

**48**

come in and read the book, we have a hot one on the line. Now the book is also jam packed with useful content as well. If you are reading this book, take note this book does *NOT* follow the sales pitch format. I am providing lots of useful information here and not pitching you something.

## *Lead Capture:*

You also need to be capturing leads as many ways as possible. You need to be collecting info and building lists all the time so we can put these people in the sales funnel.

One of my clients was hosting an annual event in which over a thousand people show up to each year. The problem is that he has no idea who they are. I gave him this advice:

**\* \* \* \* \* \* \* \* \* \***

I would fence off most of the event from the parking lot and have an entrance gate. And just give them wristbands there. When they get the wristband, someone from the family has to put their email address in. That's how you track how many people were there and everything like that. Send them a thank you email. Thanks for coming out and then you can passively follow up with them.

You've got to find a way to capture their information because then you don't have to mail the cold list anymore. You have the list. You own it and you know it is full of people who have been at the event. These are all good prospects for you.

Actually, one step better. For this event, you should start a birthday club. The little kids' names should be in there and their birthdays – and you're going to send them something on their birthday. You can send them a birthday card with a coupon a month before their birthday so they have a coupon for their party. I mean, that's gold to know when their birthday is, right?

* * * * * * * * *

# 17. Selling Face To Face

This topic is way too in-depth to give any justice in this book. I do want to say that the real high dollar transactions are usually done in a face-to-face environment either one-to-one or one-to-many. You *NEED* to develop personal selling skills and learn how to build rapport quickly and effectively. You need to learn how to get prospects to reveal their buying criteria. You need a well rehearsed sales framework and you need to stick to it. You need to learn to read body language and know what your body language says about you.

See the resource section of this book for some of my favorite sales books that you should get your hands on and study. The basic process of any sales meeting is:

1. **Build Rapport:** You must get to know your prospect and get them to like you. You need to find common ground. You need to get them comfortable with you and get them to trust you. The easiest way to do this is to ask personal questions. What they do for a living? Hobbies? Dreams? Etc. You must actually LISTEN to their answers and care about what they tell you. You need to find a way to CONNECT. People buy from people who they like and trust.

2. **Needs Analysis:** Now is time to figure out exactly what they are looking for. A consultative process is

best. You ask lots of questions to get an idea of what they like or don't like. What they may be worried about. What they are excited about. What they think they need and what they may not say that you know fits what they are looking for. Ask lots of questions, listen, and take notes. You can address concerns as they arise but now is not the time to *pitch* or talk price.

3. **Solution Presentation:** Next up is your presentation of what you offer. This is probably going to be 70% (or more) the same for each meeting, but the other 30% is the important part. The 30% is what you tweak that specifically speaks to what they told you in step 2. Make sure you focus on only what is important to them. Everything else really doesn't matter as much.

4. **Closing The Sale:** Now is the time to ask for the sale. The best path is to "prescribe" a couple of solutions based on what they told you. Once you lay out a couple options, ask them which one they like the best and then shut up. The first person to talk usually loses. You can often talk them out of a purchase now but it is too late to do more convincing. That time was earlier in the process. Be firm and confident in your presentation and ask them how to proceed.

You need to know this process inside and out and be comfortable with it. If you skip a step, you will most likely lose the sale. If you go out of order, you will most likely lose the sale. Be consistent, precise, and take notes during your face-to-face meetings. The prospects don't care how much you know until they know how much you care.

One more thing, sales ability is not something you are born with. It is a skill that can be learned by anybody. It is a mindset and practice. If at first you don't succeed, do not get discouraged. If you use all the marketing tips in this book, the actual sales job becomes fairly easy.

# 18. Selling on The Phone

Do you have a script for whoever picks up the phone? If not, now is the time to write one. While you may think you answer the same way every time, unless you have a script, I sincerely doubt you do. Each phone call needs to be consistent regardless of who answers the phone.

If somebody is calling in or you are calling out the process is the same as in face-to-face selling:

1. Build Rapport
2. Needs Analysis
3. Solution Presentation
4. Closing The Sale

If you are making outbound calls, your period of time to build rapport may be literally seconds so you better know what you are going to say the moment the other line of that phone is picked up.

Before we moved into our first commercial space, all our sales were done exclusively by phone. Outbound calls were used to setup scheduled consultations (sales calls). I would regularly book $1,200 to $3,000 contracts off of 30-50 minute phone calls without the client ever seeing our company in action or meeting with me or anyone else physically. Complete the 4 steps in the sales call and get the credit card number at the end. It works! That being said, you can stack a lot more items in your favor in a face-to-face environment when you consider as much as 90% of our communication is nonverbal (meaning you can't see it over the phone). Even better is you can control the environment.

# 19. Selling In Print

If you are good selling face-to-face or on the phone, it is easy to transition to selling in print. You've just got to figure out how to transfer those skills over. It's just going to be a matter of downloading your brain onto paper and then making it appear in the right format. There is also a slightly different basic marketing formula used in making customers take action. This is: A.I.D.A.

**Attention:** The first step is to get the prospect's attention. Fail at this and the rest doesn't matter.

**Interest:** Once you have their attention, you have to interest them more. You have to draw them into your story. You must speak to them directly.

**Desire:** The next step is to make them want what you have to offer.

**Action:** Finally, you need to make them take action. Spell out specifically how they are supposed to respond and what they need to do next.

## *Brochures*

The brochures are what I like to call *feel good* pieces. I don't think a whole lot of decisions are made out of them, but sometimes they are a necessary evil because people are used to them. They want to see them. It says, *Hey, I'm a legit business, I got a brochure.* Sometimes you got to play that game.

If you feel you must have an image brochure then mail it in an envelope with a letter enclosed. The letter should have a little explanation of what you want them to do. *Have a look at the enclosed brochure, give me a call, we have this going on right now.* I realize it's going to cost a little more because now they got to go out in an envelope, but it'll be worth it.

The brochures that have done the most good in my business are for the Photo Booth Services we offer. We mailed them to hotels. If there's a literature rack somewhere you want to be in, unfortunately you have to send a brochure. If you are at a tradeshow where everyone has a brochure, you need to have something different to stand out. Whatever you do, make sure your brochure follows the AIDA formula and has some sort of call to action. It needs to tell the reader what they are supposed to do next.

# 20. Selling With Direct Mail

Direct mail is considered dead by many online marketers but I am here to tell you the direct mail can be one the best, most effective advertising media out there if you use it correctly. Printing and mailing can be done fairly cheaply but the best part of using direct mail is your ability to target exactly who is most likely to respond and mail just to them. It is far more targeted than putting an ad on the TV or radio and more effective for 99.9% of businesses. You can put only those people on your mailing list who are going to make you money.

If you are new to direct mail, you may be wondering:

Where do I get a list? Who should be on the list? What do I do with it once I have it?. Sound familiar?

The best possible list is to generate your own − a warm one but barring that one can always be purchased as well. Generating your own list is what you should be doing on your websites. How do we do this? It goes back to lead generation marketing, meaning these aren't hard offers going out like book us and get this. It's something that they're going to raise their hand and say, *Yes, I want more information.* It's that non-confrontational thing.

I'll give you an example from one of our businesses. For our corporate game show marketing for holiday parties, we mail post cards. The post card has a client testimonial. Obviously, there are a lot of testimonials from the most recognizable names I have in my client database. The postcard asks them to call for their free corporate planning information kit that has this report on how to hire this and checklists to make sure that you're planning your event properly.

So they're not calling for promotional info, although it is in there. They get mailed a game show corporate planning package, but it has all this other stuff that they want as well. This helps when someone is a little more passive. They're not necessarily looking for your service right now, but they are planning an event. And even when they're planning that event, they're a good lead for us because they have the ability to book us eventually

The package they receive in the mail (not via email) comes in a priority mail envelope and contains a nice presentation folder and has like 20 or 30 pages of reports, 10 pages of promo materials. It has a CD in there with a couple of Excel files for them. Basically, I'm trying to give them as much as I can. In my wedding business, it's my book along with all that other stuff in there.

We're going to test (sometime this year) sending them a bound book with 200 customer testimonials that says, *You need proof, here it is*. Just something that once they open it, it's all over their desk, just everywhere. And then they call back and you can walk them through the process.

At that point, it's back to a sales call, which is what you're doing. Everything is trying to drive them back into a call asking specifically about the service. I would let them know I will be including custom price quotes and that allows me to ask a lot of questions about the event like: Who have you hired in the past? What have you done? This process can be duplicated in any type of business you may have.

*The Initial List.* You have to really know beyond a shadow of a doubt who your client is, how they think, where they work, and how big the company is. Many of my consulting clients kind of struggle with this ideal client concept. You have to take the time to study your clients and find the commonalities. If you need to call and interview 20 past clients, do it. Once you find common characteristics, you can search for lists of people that match those characteristics.

## A-Pile vs. B-Pile

When someone opens their mailbox, they often immediately sort their mail into what marketers call A-pile and B-pile mail. A-pile mail is personal mail: letters, greeting cards, invitations, etc. B-pile mail is most likely going straight in the garbage.People get their mail and sort it over the garbage can. The A-pile, I'm keeping, and the B-pile's just gone without even a chance. It is very important that you make your mail appear like A-pile personal mail if you want it to get opened.

The postcard gives you a benefit because they don't have to open an envelope. They actually looked at your message. If you send something under an envelope, they can throw it away without seeing your message.

You've got to segment it down and only advertise what you're thinking is the most relevant thing for that person you're sending it to. This can be difficult to figure out but once you do, fortunes have been built on one effective letter or postcard.

# *Getting It Read*

The first challenge is getting it read. Once it's opened, that's good. But we've got to get further than that. You need to make sure you have a good headline or hook. If your headline sucks, the rest of your letter doesn't stand a chance because they aren't going to read that far.

Telling stories is another way to keep them reading. Relevant business or personal stories always interest people but the headline is what will make them read the story. The same is true of magazines at the grocery store checkout isle. Next time you are there take a look at some of the headlines. They are written by some of the best marketers in the world.

You also need to write for what is called "dual readership path." Basically, the concept is that there are two different ways that people will read what is written. One type of person will read every word. The second type will skim, reading only headlines, bolded words, headings, pictures, and captions. You need to make sure that if someone is skimming, they will still be able to understand your whole message. Make sure you read your letter both ways before sending it.

## Timing Your Mailings

The next fatal flaw of small business owners is mailing something once and being done. You want to mail at least three times. The problem is how closely do you mail together. Too soon and they get annoyed. Too far apart and we lose effectiveness.

The idea of basic advertising campaign is a sequence of 3 letters based 10-14 days apart. Each letter refers back to the one that was sent before it. It says, *I sent you this letter and haven't heard back from you.* This is very similar to what a collection company would send you. The third letter is often stamped "Final Notice" at the top even.

## Grabbers

The only other thing I have space to share with you about mailing is that sometimes you attach what's called a *grabber*, some sort of 3D item. For instance, often times ad specialty companies will mail a pen in an envelope. When you get that envelope and feel something in there you just have to open it to see what it is. Another common one is a single packet of Aspirin, often with a headline of _____ *giving you a headache? We can help.* It seems silly but it gets response.

# 21. Selling Online

The first thing I want to share about online advertising is that it is way overhyped. It is important but it is not the "end-all be-all" of marketing. If you want evidence of that fact, how many times a year do you get an advertisement in the mail from Google offering free ad words credit? If you are already running a business, chances are you get them all the time.

Every time you see one of these letters, it is kind of a validation that you can't start eliminating direct mail. Google can advertise all day long for free on their search engine but they have chosen to mail millions of pieces of advertising in physical postal mail. They are not stupid so you can rest assured it is profitable for them to do so.

## *Social Media Marketing*

This section was revised within a week of publishing due to a major change in Facebook advertising. Up until this point, Facebook was basically a popularity contest and it was very, very difficult to justify time and effort spent to get *'likes'* and similar interaction. In fact, you can hire people oversees with bogus Facebook accounts to click *'Like'* and have 5,000 new likes within 24 hours.

It is pretty difficult to get a return off of paid Facebook

ads – it really is. It is worth adding posts when you have nothing else going on. It is also powerful for event of photo driven businesses.

The big kicker that just unveiled was that Facebook now has teamed up with major data and list providers that allows you to target ads much deeper than you could before. You can now target by household income, type of car owned, and a ton of other things that you never knew that Facebook knows about you. Facebook is lining up their account profiles with known mailing list profiles. This is very important and a game changer for anyone that "knows their customer" in enough details to be able to target them with pinpoint accuracy under available criteria.

## Google Adwords

Google is still the leading search engine by far and we do personally get a ton of business from Google Adwords. Our data says as much as 40% of one of our business divisions comes from paid adwords.

*Adwords* are paid advertisements within search engines. So you are going to bid on terms like, "Dallas", "Pest Control" and when somebody searches for those terms, Google will show your ad somewhere. It depends on how much you bid, where it is at, and how many people click on it. Needless to say, it has to be a good ad.

But the thing is, if you have the right keywords, there are

good buyers. For instance, you could tell it to not show your ad when someone types the word *"cheap"* or *"lowest price."* So if it was important to you to not spend money on those people, you could tell Google that fact and your ad will not show for those keywords. You can also do it by geography, which is very important to local service businesses. You can say, "Hey, only show this ad to people within 30 miles of Orlando, Florida."

Google doesn't have a lot of demographic targeting ability like Facebook does. However, usually someone searching for your keywords on Google is a more likely buyer than somebody talking to their friends on Facebook. You have to think, "What is someone going to type in the Google box when they are looking to hire a company like yours?"

# 22. Email Marketing

When we advertise via email, we have to be aware of certain laws, as well as several other things that can stop your emails from being delivered. One of the most important is people clicking complain or spam when they get your e-mail. If too many people do this, then when you send an email nobody will ever see it. It will go straight to everybody's spam or junk mail folder. Make sure anything you email is requested and of interest to the people who are receiving it. Do not send information on snow cone makers to somebody who requested a free report on muscle cars.

You also need to provide a way for your recipients to opt-out or unsubscribe from future emails. We don't care if they opt out, but when they click *'spam'*, it causes all your other e-mails to start having trouble getting delivered. If somebody opts out of a relevant message, it is clear they are not interested in what you have to offer and you should not be wasting time, money, or effort to change their mind.

The other important thing is the frequency of the e-mails have to be consistent. I know marketers that email every day to their lists, and ones that e-mail every month. I would lean towards monthly or maybe every couple of months. Make sure it's consistent. That way they know what to expect.

Otherwise, if they go 6 months and they don't get an email and then suddenly get one, they'll probably hit spam because they might not remember signing up for it. People receive tons of email and it is not their job to remember what they signed up for. They either want your email or they don't.

There's some other things going on in the e-mail marketing world as this book is being published that's making it even more difficult to get your messages read. With G-Mail in particular, over the last month and a half they have been phasing in a tabbed view of e-mail meaning they're automatically separating user's e-mail into a main e-mail box, a social media e-mail box, and a promotions e-mail box.

So if you are using an email software, everything's going to go to that promotions tab. We've yet to see how that's going to affect people but based on my behavior alone, I don't think it's good because I know that I delete a lot more than I used to. I used to read them. So it's getting hard to even get your e-mail read.

For people who have Yahoo email accounts, in the last month they have launched something where they're penalizing you if you e-mail inactive or old accounts. Meaning if you have a Yahoo account in your e-mail list and the person hasn't logged on to their account in 4 months, they consider it inactive. And if you send emails to a bunch of those, they're going to slow down the delivery to the legit ones going to Yahoo addresses.

There's a massive battle going on right now. And it's yet

to be seen what's going to happen with e-mail. But it's getting harder to use and be effective at.

Yeah, I know. It's another Catch-22. If you send too much, you get spam complaints; you don't send enough and you get spam complaints. You've got to find middle ground.

## *Nurture Sequences:*

At some point, you probably want to look into setting up an automated email nurture sequence. There are a lot of people who, regardless of what you say, aren't going to book immediately or when they initially contact you so it's good to have a formal system to keep in contact rather than a sporadic round of emails. It's called a nurture sequence. It's a little work to set up but once you set it up, it's automated. For instance, our nurture sequence for DJ services is 18 months long right now. They're going to get weekly emails for a year and a half unless I hear from them otherwise.

I don't just send a bunch of sales pitch emails. I educate them about the service. I educating them about other things going on. So when they're actually looking to make that decision they remember to call us again and then we can put them back in the top of the sales funnel and start the sales process over.

# 23. Other Marketing Media

## *Event Marketing:*

In many different businesses, special events can be used for marketing. These may be open houses, tent sales, tradeshows, family and friends days, or a myriad of other events that draw crowds. When you host an expensive event like this, it is important to do everything you can to capitalize on it. The first step is to capture information from everyone there. The second step is sorting legitimate leads from curious people. The easiest way to capture event leads is to offer a sign-up for a giveaway. The key to the second step is to make your giveaway be something that only would be of interest to somebody that may be in need of your product or service.

## *Text Messaging:*

In some event settings, it would be more advantageous to set up a text messaging system. You're going to have to give them something to get them to text it. They're not going to do it for free. You're not going to be able to force it on them. Most people love texting but they won't do it just for fun. Offer free content or a discount coupon that is sent back immediately when somebody joins your text list.

## *Chamber of Commerce:*

A lot of businesses join a local chamber of commerce

thinking that all of a sudden new business will just pour in. It doesn't happen that way. The second flaw is thinking they can just attend meetings and give away as many business cards as possible and those people will call. Also, not true.

The problem is that it's not something you join and get business. It's something you really have to put time and effort into to get anything out of it. Yeah, it's like building relationships (because you are) and it's slow going. You can't come in with a stack of business cards to a morning meeting and start pitching. It won't get you anywhere. You can't go in with a sales attitude. You have to go in with a what can I do to help attitude and give it time.

Often times, chamber members will do business with their chamber friends before other people. Once you're in there and you volunteer for stuff, they do actually think of chamber members first. Especially if you put them on your monthly newsletter after you meet them.

The only other thing I can say is that if you join, ask how you can get involved. Most of the people are going to write the check and never do anything. So be that person that harasses the staff a little bit and tries to maximize it and they'll help you.

# 24. Publicity & TV Appearances

Many people think that if they could just get on TV, then people will see them and they will be rich. Although there are exceptions, that's not usually the case. Just appearing on the TV is kind of cool but it's not going to do much for your business on its own.

It's what you do afterwards to exploit that appearance. Here are a couple of quick tips for media appearances.

1. Make sure you have a *'newsworthy'* story to get on TV in the first place

2. Make sure you have a lead generation magnet to offer for viewers and a website setup to collect leads

3. Make sure you get permission to record and use the segment for whatever you wish

4. Make sure you use the media logos and appearance video everywhere you can to show people that you were on TV. You will be amazed how powerful it is and a 60 second appearance can live on and benefit you for years.

I typically do not recommend paid TV or radio ads for most small businesses. They are very costly and the money can be better spent in other areas. Once your other campaigns are in place and profitable, then you may want to look into broadcast media to compliment those current campaigns but not as a standalone promotion. Let me give you a personal example:

Around 2001, my company launched a business called 'The Element Mobile Nightclub' which was to be a travelling dance party for teenagers. Our media strategy was just plain dumb looking back but sounded good. We basically owned the airwaves of the only local top 40 radio station for about 2 weeks leading up to the launch. This was also at a time prior to the popularity of satellite and streaming radio so many more people were listening than now. I think in all we spent about $4,000 and did little else to attract customers. The results of constant radio ads for two weeks to our target demographic? Less than 50 people showed up. It was a total loss but a major learning lesson to be careful with perception of media versus the reality of it.

# 25. Tactical Promotions & Sales

In this chapter, we will focus on running one-time special offers or promotions with a specific end goal in mind. Usually when you run a special promotions, you have to tie them to something in order for them to be effective. There has to be a reason for the sale. Holidays are some of the best and most effective events to build promotions around. Some of the favorites in my business are 3-day weekend holidays such as Memorial Day and Labor Day. These holidays are on the top of people's minds as they are already planning special activities during them. The 4th of July as well as Black Friday have also been very effective for us. For a couple years, I have even run a *"it's my wife's birthday and I forgot to budget for her present"* campaign.

Oftentimes, promotions like this are great when you need an instant cash surge or when you have a number of potential buyers sitting on the fence and you need to give them a good kick in the pants to act right now.

Promoting these sale events can be as simple as sending a couple emails and a postcard or two. They can lead to tens of thousands of dollars in quick sales. To be effective at this, you need to try and have some incentive. Usually it is just as effective to add on a bonus rather than give a discount though. So for instance, the wife's birthday promotion is actually promoting one of our highest priced packages but I throw in some additional incentives that have a high perceived value but do not cost me that much to fulfill on. I don't like to just give away money. Discounts off the price are you giving up pure profit. Keep that in mind as you decide what incentives will work best for you.

It is important to limit your sales and not always be having a sale. Otherwise, your prospects will learn to just keep waiting and there will be another sale coming. So you have got to be careful, especially if you have repeat clients. You don't want to train them to wait for something that they know is coming up. One way around this is to allow current and repeat clients in on a sale if they refer a friend that hires us.

## Bounce Back Coupons

A bounce back coupon is a popular promotion where when somebody comes to your business or buys something you give them a coupon that is only valid at a future date. This way they have to come back to the store again and start to develop a habit of shopping with you. It works in tons of industries from retail to bars and can be adapted for pretty much anything. In fact, today my wife and I are headed to Kohl's department store to use some Kohl's Cash. This is one of their bounce back promotions. Try to think of how you can incorporate this into your business and get your customers to buy more often.

## *Souvenirs*

Sometimes a nickel of investment can yield dollars of sales. It is very powerful to be able to give your customers something totally for free. One of the foremost examples I can think of is that my church gives guests a free water bottle and some candy with no strings attached. Restaurants often give away samples. An experience focused business can give away photos. The possibilities are endless. If you can find something to give that includes your name, it can yield good results. The items must be related to what you do and they must be given out without any strings. I am convinced that at a local barbecue *'Ribfest'* I attended, the people's choice winner won solely because they were the only participant giving out stickers to everyone. It probably cost them two cents a piece but worked wonders for them and they had a line all day. Don't underestimate the power of this tactic.

# 26. Testing & Tracking with Absolute Accuracy

I would consider this chapter to probably be the most important one in the entire book. You need to know how to track (with absolute certainty) every piece of advertising you put out. If you are not tracking, you are just gambling. It's often said that 50% of ad dollars are wasted and if you could just figure out which 50% you were wasting, you would be rich. This statement is foolish because with direct response advertising, you can – and you had better be tracking everything.

The basic concept of how to track is pretty simple. If the ad wants people to go online, each ad sends them to a different web address and you can check how many people visited each site. If you want them to call, each ad has a different tracking phone number. My company has somewhere between 30 and 40 website addresses and probably 30-40 phone numbers too. Advertising is expensive. Website urls and phone numbers are cheap in comparison.

Every time I spend money on an advertisement, I am always sure it can be tracked. For example, if I were sending two thousand postcards out, they would have a special phone number and a special web address on it that I could easily track. So I would know exactly how many calls came from this particular postcard and exactly how many people went to the website on it. Then I know if this is not effective, I never send it again – or at a minimum, I tweak it and test it all over again.

I did the same thing with all the phone books, and all the yellow pages ads. Every book had a different phone number in it. I got like 3 calls a year off some of the books, and 2 of them were my competitors. I was able to quickly and confidently drop that advertising campaign. Not to mention, it was very amusing listening to the ad rep try to come up with a good reason to advertise with them when facing absolute fact.

I can positively say that I didn't get any business from those phone books for that business. That knowledge has allowed me to free up  and save thousands of dollars each year. That money can be put to better use elsewhere. My cost to track with a special phone number and everything was only $10 or less a month. And I only have to keep the number for 1 year to figure out if it's working or not. It is a bargain.

The only way to know for sure is to test and track. There's no silver bullet, it's test and track. Testing without tracking is pointless. You might be able to hit some good numbers but if we don't know exactly where they're coming from, we can't reproduce it over and over and your business will never grow. You will just have random good times and bad times. Knowing this strategy and implementing it is how you take control of your business profitability.

# 27. Maximizing Referrals

Referrals are the lifeblood of many businesses and are absolutely the best and cheapest way to build you business. Unfortunately, too many business owners leave referrals to chance. It is your job to train your customers to refer and to build a culture of referring fans.

There are three basic rules for getting customers to refer:

**1: Encourage & Ask for Referrals:** You need to make it a habit to ask each and every customer if they know anybody else that may be in need of your services. You also need to remind them every once in awhile that your business depends on referrals and the majority of new customers come from referrals. Finally, you must give them the tools to refer. Print up some *referral business cards* with a special discount they can hand out their friends.

**2: Recognize Referrers:** When somebody refers a friend to you, it is your job to recognize them for doing so. At a minimum, send them a hand-written thank you card. Public recognition is even better (see the next section on newsletters, my favorite referral building tool).

**3: Rewards Referrers:** You should also reward people for this behavior. Be careful with this so that they do not see it as an outright bribe. How big the reward is depends on how big your average sale is. In my company, it is a box of fresh baked cookies for them and $50.00 off for the person they referred. If you do not reward the behavior it will stop occurring. Do not leave referrals to chance!

## Using Newsletters to Build Referrals:

Here is another tip that can literally change your business. My number one tool for increasing referrals is to send a monthly PRINT (not email) newsletter to all my current and past clients.

One of the most read sections of this newsletter is the *Client of the Month.* It keeps those past clients looking again because: (A) they want to see if it's them and (B) they want to see if they know the person. We also print a list of all our new clients and all the past month's referrers.

One important note on designing your newsletter is that you should not make it all about you! If you are a realtor, the newsletter can't just be about houses. It's got to be fun and entertaining. If I send out a 4-page newsletter that's all about me, they're going to throw it away. They don't care.

Our newsletter has personal stories about what is going on in my life (outside of work), crossword puzzles, horoscopes, and plenty of jokes and comics. In the 10 years we've been doing this, I can't tell you how many times I get stopped at other businesses and out and about with people telling me, "We get your newsletter and we love it." People actually do read it because it's entertaining. It's not a blatant sales pitch. Just the fact it's on their desk and getting read is the pitch.

*Who should you mail to?* Every single past client you've ever had. If you have hot prospects you really want, you put them on there. Anyone that can refer you business. That's a big one. We get 30% of our business from vendor referrals, not customer referrals. We get another 25% from customer referrals. My family's on there. Honestly, anyone that may refer stays on the list. If it's a past client and they don't refer for 3 years, we remove them from the mailing list at that point.

## Post Fulfillment Follow-Up

Another good way to build up referring clients is the process you go through after your product or service has been delivered. A  phone call is a good start. I suggest mailing out a survey or posting an online survey that gets sent out after EVERY transaction.

I suggest using a two-page survey or feedback form. The first page of our feedback form doesn't dig very deep. It is some basic questions and a spot for a testimonial. We use this page in our book of testimonials and customer feedback as a sales tool for future clients.

The second page is actually much more important and should include:

**Top 3 concerns you had before you hired us.** The

reason that you care about this is that it's telling you why people are picking one company over another. This is the buying criteria. What are they worried about? This information is gold because it lets you write future ads addressing only what is important to the actual customers.

**Top 3 Things You Liked About Us.** This is telling you what you're good at and it's hopefully giving you something usable as a testimonial. Or, you can even word it as, *Please give your testimonial on what you liked about us*, and then you have those quotes to use.

The third question, is where they'd be asked, **Don't worry about hurting our feelings; please tell us what specific things we can change to improve our business.** A lot of the times we will get some input from this question. If it wasn't worded that way, they'll probably never tell us if something was only bothering them a little bit. So, we've got to let them know to be brutally honest and give us something. 10 or 20 of those "little" ideas can be the difference between having a successful business and failing. It's the little things that matter.

# 28. Basic Pricing Strategy

All we have room for in this book is a crash course on pricing strategy so I will share what I know and what has worked for us. In most businesses, you can make a conscious decision to pursue pricing as the cheapest, middle, or most expensive relative to your competitors.

Let's look at being the lowest cost provider first. This is a VERY difficult position to operate a business in. Often, it leaves razor thin margins and not much room for mistakes before you are bankrupt. It is also a game that is near impossible to win as somebody else will always try to be cheaper. It will go back and forth until there is no money left for anyone. Suffice it to say that I am not a fan of this strategy at all. It is usually pursued by inexperienced business owners or ones that are scared and think that people only buy what is cheap and they will lose business by raising their prices. Mathematically, you could double your prices and lose half your business and be in the same spot. Actually, you would be in a better spot because your fulfillment costs would be cut in half as well. Unless you are Wal-Mart, you will not win the low cost game. (An interesting side note is that they are even having difficulty as Amazon.com eats away at their business).

Let's talk about a middle of the road pricing strategy.

This is where most companies fall. That means to you that this is also the strategy that has the most competition. It is very hard to differentiate your business from that of your competitor if you both have middle prices. This (more than anything else) will cause your potential customer to start comparing on the basis of price. This is often considered the most dangerous spot to be.

Now let's talk about my favorite place to be, high-end pricing. There are so many advantages to being high priced (or even the highest priced) that it is ridiculous. I will name just a few. First, is the obvious one that more money is coming in with each sale. Second, is that customers will have a perception of you being the best based on nothing more than you being the most expensive. Third, you probably can be the best because you have more funds coming in to spend on fulfilling your obligations to your clients. You don't need to cut corners. Next, the numbers are much more forgiving. You don't need to get as many customers in the first place. Should a refund be due, it won't kill you. Unexpected bill? No problem. Tried a couple ads and they didn't work? We'll make it up on the next one. Probably the single biggest advantage is that you can "spend" more to get a customer. You can afford to advertise more and do more things to get traffic in the door. One other dirty little secret is that the customers that spend more money are often the easiest to work for (with some notable exceptions).

# 29. Handling Price Objections

After reading the last chapter, a lot of you are probably thinking that your business is different. Your clients are cheap and won't pay top dollar. You would go out of business if you raised prices. Guess what, the problem probably isn't the pricing, it's your sales and marketing ability. For this reason, I am going to include a little here about how to handle pricing objections. Realize, you won't be able to convince everyone. Thankfully, you don't have to in order to have a very profitable business.

So what do you do when someone calls and the first thing out of their mouth is, "How much is xyz?" The simple answer is don't answer the question and take control of the call. Basically, the person asking the questions is the one that is controlling the call and you need to take that position.

Here is the best technique I have for that question. We actually respond with a question. "Is price the only thing you're concerned about?" If they say yes, then say, "We're probably not the best company for you. Thanks." Just let it go. You can't turn that person around. They're a jerk and you don't need the stress. Even if you did manage to get their business, you would regret it later.

If they say, no (which most will), then they've opened up the door and now we've got time for the sales pitch. You can ask them what else is of concern to them. That's when they will tell you their hiring criteria. They're going to lay it out for you and then you can respond with the appropriate things that they told you.

It turns the conversation around really quickly. Sometimes they don't know what to ask besides what the price is. They've never hired a service like yours before. They have no clue what they should be asking. They think it's all the same. It's up to you to educate the customer.

If you take control and turn the conversation around then you can begin the sales process we laid out earlier in this book for sales meetings or you can invite them to schedule a meeting with you to go over all of their concerns in detail. Do not fall into the trap that all people care about is the price. It is simply not true. Study sales and you will learn countless other techniques used to deal with *price shoppers*.

# 30. Dealing With Demanding Clients

One of the benefits of offering premium priced services is that the clients are usually very nice. If they are not, often times you can feel great about turning down their business as you don't have to have them as a client. This is a very liberating feeling when you exercise this option. Sometimes though, you just have to know how to deal with very assertive clients. Basically, you need to match their energy level and take control of the situation. I can best illustrate this through an example from my wedding business.

We had a mother of a bride call into the office looking for information on wedding services and wanted to know a price without offering any information. She was relentlessly pounding my sales rep for a price (which there is actually no way for him to give accurately without asking a ton of questions).

And he's sticking to his guns. He's not allowed to say a price on the phone in this particular sales process. They have to come in the office for a consultation so we can diagnose how to best serve them and the associated price. And she gets nowhere and frustrated, so then he ends the call and says he'll call her back with some info.

He comes crawling to my office. What do I do? She doesn't want to come in. She's really busy. I'm like, well, that's too bad. Tell her she has to come in.

So he calls her back and is still unsuccessful on this second call. So I have to get on the phone at this point. He hasn't had all the sales training I have so it's not his fault. He doesn't have all the experience. So I get her on the phone. I do exactly the same approach. I ask, is price the only thing you're worried about? Well no. It's a wedding and there are a ton of other things that are important as well.

Well, it's important you come in to our office so we can sit down and see how to best help you. I'm not even sure I can provide what you want [this is a key phrase as well and catches the prospect off guard]. I'm not even sure if I'm the right person for you. But if you come in we can sit down and look through your plans. I guarantee I won't waste your time. But we have to do that to see if we can even proceed further. And then I can get you a price.

Guess what? She came in and did the same thing in the meeting. We had to spin it around again. And finally, she ends up booking a high-priced package.

You see, she asked about price but it really wasn't her primary concern. She is just used to being in charge and you have to take control of that process.

It's not uncommon for someone like that to call. Honestly, when you deal with people high up on the corporate ladder, they're used to just delegating and telling people what to do. You've got to get them out of that role and be on a level playing field with them. You have to get respect as a peer, not a subordinate. At that point and only at that point will you stand a chance of building a real business relationship and end up with a happy client. If after all that, they still insist on being demanding then you have a decision to make. If the money matters the most to you, you can take the job knowing what you are likely getting in to. If the principle matters more, you can simply turn down the work and move on to the next prospect.

# 31. Using Takeaway Selling

One of the things you may have noticed in the last chapter was that I used *takeaway selling*. The basic premise of takeaway selling is that people want what they cannot have. It is basic human nature and you can use it to your advantage. You need to include some sort of urgency into your sales process so the prospect gets the feeling they may miss out. If you have a true capacity issue like we do, then it is easy. If someone else books us on their special day, we will be unavailable for them. It is first-come, first-served and I am often able to honestly tell them that there are 40 or more other couples in our sales system with the same date as theirs.

Take a moment right now to think about how you can use takeaway selling as opposed to "pushing" people into buying.

# 32. Your Marketing Calendar

By this point in the book, you probably have at least a handful of different things you want to implement immediately. That or you have become so overwhelmed you have no idea where to begin and how you can possibly manage it all when you are already so busy. A successful company always has a lot going on and oftentimes there will be several different projects going on at the same time. One tool that many successful business owners use is called the marketing calendar.

The marketing calendar is exactly what is sounds like. It is a one year calendar that spells out each promotion and advertising piece you are going to use and when you are going to use them. It should also have other deadlines before each advertisement for any other items needing completion that may cause you to miss your deadline if you forget them (new designs, printing, tracking setup, etc).

The marketing calendar can be as simple as an Excel file sorted by date or my personal favorite if you are a more visual person is to buy one of those 2' x 3' laminated wall calendars. I then use both markers as well as colored dot stickers to plan out everything.

While the idea of a marketing calendar may seem really simple, please do not brush this off as useless. This is often the only way to make sure things get done and you should get started on making your marketing calendar right away.

If you decide to skip this step, you will likely run into problems. What will happen is that shortly after you start a new promotion, you will get busy serving the customers that the promotion brought in. Two or three months pass and then you are slow on customers again and the bank account balance nears zero because you were "too busy" to market. You then run another marketing piece and repeat the cycle all over again. This is all too common and can easily be avoided if you have a marketing calendar planned out in advance and you stick to it knowing it is of vital importance.

# 33. Scaling Your Business

Here's where it gets exciting. If you are able to implement what you learned here and create an advertisement that yields qualified prospects and you know beyond a shadow of a doubt where they came from, then growing your business is easy. It is simply a matter of placing the winning ad multiple times until it stops producing for you. At some point, your business problems won't revolve around getting clients but will revolve around fulfillment. This is the point these techniques have allowed my entertainment business to get to. It is not a matter of bringing in clients, it is a matter of making sure we don't take on more business than we can satisfy to the fullest quality.

It's the same basic process whether your average sale is $200 or $20,000. Growing and scaling your business will bring about a host of other challenges but marketing won't be the bottleneck anymore. If the thought of multiplying your client base isn't exciting to you, you should probably get out of business. I sincerely wish the best for you and a host of new problems (in a good way).

# 34. Using Outside Contractors & Consultants

Okay, so now we have the marketing campaigns conceived, the marketing calendar of when they need to happen, and a clear game plan for the business. At this point, life is going to happen. You are all set and ready to go and you will get really busy either in your business or your personal life. It's perfectly normal, but it can threaten your business growth plans.

The good news is you don't have to do it all alone. Unless you have absolutely no cash (in which case you probably have time on your hands) you can find quality people to help you at reasonable prices. If you are fortunate, you may already have staff you can delegate some of this to. If not, you may be able to hire an intern from a local college.

Finally, you could use my favorite method which is to hire specialized contractors. You may be thinking this will cost you a fortune, but it really doesn't if you know where to look. In the resources section of this book, you will find several websites we use to look for contractors. The services you can outsource are amazing. Some that we have hired in the past are: graphic design, web design, video editing, transcription, editing, web research, data entry, telemarketing, personal assistants, and countless others. You name it and it can be outsourced.

Regardless of if you have a staff member or a contractor working with you, you need to make sure you manage the process. You can't tell someone to do something and then forget about it. If you do, guess what? It probably won't get done. You need to own this process and stay involved. Your business depends on it.

# 35. Continuing Your Education

My thoughts on formal college education are probably going to surprise quite a few people. On the wall behind my desk are three college degrees: including an Associate's Degree, a Bachelor's Degree, and a Master's Degree in Business Administration. Despite all of this formal education, I still insist that my most important and valuable lessons were learned in actually running my business. I have a massive problem with learning from, and being graded by, business professors that have never actually operated a business on their own. While academic research is valuable, it's not the most beneficial activity for a business to partake in. I also believe that you may be better served by going to business school a little later in life after you have some working experience.

While business school was good at teaching overall philosophies of managing a business, what it lacked was nuts and bolts tactics of how to get things done, such as what I'm sharing in this book. If you want exposure to a variety of different business topics ranging from accounting, finance, marketing, management, and even ethics, then business school is the place for you. However, if you are most concerned with getting a business running, getting profits in the door, and not worried about figuring out things as you go, then forgoing the schooling is oftentimes a shortcut to success.

With that in mind, I will say that I'm a massive fan of lifelong learning. I have several bookshelves full of books on business that I've learned from. I've attended countless workshops all around the country to continue to develop my skills further. I spend tens of thousands of dollars every year on getting new ideas and help from other people. While formal education focuses on what the college considers to be important for the curriculum, when you are choosing what workshops and books to read and seminars to attend you can pick what is most important to you at any particular given time in your business. You don't need to waste time on things that are irrelevant to you at that point in time. You can focus on the things that are going to produce the best return for your investment of time and money and you will actually learn and retain the information better because of it.

In the resource directory of this book, you will see a suggested reading list of books that have been tremendous contributors to my success. I would also highly, highly encourage you to attend one of my one-day business acceleration boot camps. In just one day, I promise to cover more material that will bring you more dollars than an entire master's degree in college would. That being said, you need to come focused and ready to learn. You also need to block out time upon your return to your company to actually sit down and digest what you learned and begin implementation. More information on upcoming boot camps is available on the website listed in the resource directory of this book.

"Formal education will make you a living; self-education will make you a fortune."

· *Jim Rohn*

# 36. Final Thoughts

You can't implement it all right away. You've got to pick and choose what can help you the most and do that first. I can assure you that the processes I've laid out in the book can and will work for you if you actually take action. It is up to you to take those first steps right now. Make a commitment to yourself that it's time to make a change. It is time to take the *business* of your business more seriously. Take a moment to write down the first two things you are going to do and a deadline you want them done by. Those that actually do this will be the ones that see success. Those of you that read this and like the idea but don't get out that pen right now will likely just continue going about your day-to-day life. You will be a little wiser but without taking action, it means nothing. There are a lot of smart poor people. Don't be one of them.

There will be setbacks. There will be failures. That is completely normal. Don't let them ruin you. Keep moving forward. Keep your eye on your goals. You will go where you have your sight set. The journey is just beginning. Good luck!

# Bonus: Designing Your Ad

Here are a few tips on writing a profitable ad:

Anytime you write an ad, make sure it's only selling one thing and that there's only one thing you want the reader to do based on that ad. You could want them to go to a website; you could want them to call. Make sure it's very clear what you want them to do and tell them exactly how to do it.

Does it have to be pretty? I have some very ugly black and white post cards printed on yellow cardstock that make more money than my nice, glossy, professional produced graphic ones (in the wedding market nonetheless).

I hesitated for many years to even mail them because I thought they were unprofessional. Eventually, I decided that making money was more professional. I suggest you do the same sooner rather than later. The moral of the story is, you don't know until you test.

All advertisements must have some sort of offer and call to action. The offer doesn't necessarily have to be, we want to sell you something. It can be, call for information or call for a free planning session, etc.

Every offer you make has to be time-sensitive. There has to be some sort of deadline on it. If there's no deadline, it's not an ad. It's going to get put aside by the reader and eventually trashed. The deadline or restriction could be a date.

It could be a limited quantity of whatever you are offering. It has to sound like a realistic limitation that is going to make the client take action now. When they're gone, they're gone. Check out some of the quick tips below from our ad design checklist.

## The Ultimate Ad Design Checklist:

- The headline is the most important part of your ad. Without a strong headline, the rest will never be looked at.

- The P.S. at the end of the ad (for sales letters) is often the second thing to be looked at. Be sure to restate your offer in the P.S.

- Pictures can be extremely important and the captions are just as powerful as the actual pictures. Take care to find appropriate images that match your message and are memorable

- All ads should have different phone numbers and websites for response. This is so you can track with absolute certainty.

- Avoid putting a "laundry list" in your ad. This is a list of 10 different services you offer. Focus each ad on one service.

- Include social proof. Testimonials, recognized images, media logos, etc.

- Always make an offer and have an explicit call to action.

- Always have a deadline and sense of urgency

# FREE CEO SECRETS DVDs

The following three sections are portions of interviews I conducted with highly successful CEOs. As a buyer of this book, you are entitled to 3 FREE* DVDs with these interviews in their entirety. They are packed with powerful advice from people that are making things happen!

Get your 3 FREE* DVDs now at:

**www.ceosecretsdvds.com/secret/book.html**

*Just cover the shipping and handling.*

# Bonus CEO Interview Excerpt:

## *"HAPPY JOE" WHITTY*

*Founder of Happy Joe's Pizza & Ice Cream. Inventor of Taco Pizza*

We started in 1972 on November 16th. I remember the day. I remember putting the key in the door and saying, "This is mine." I remember being short on cash. I had maybe $600.

All I wanted was one little store that my wife, kids, and I could run. If I could make $40K a year, I was going to be tickled pink. That's all I asked for. The day we opened, I called a Catholic priest friend of mine and I said, "Come on down, give this place a little blessing. I think I'm going to need all the help I can get." I understand that the guy up there would work free.

So I kind of put my faith in that guy and opened the door. I prayed that people would walk in. And every day it got busier and busier, without promotion or anything.

I was working at the store one Saturday night and somebody asked, "Are you going to franchise this?"

I thought it sounded like a good idea but I had no plans to franchise it. They had said, "We'll be interested to buy a franchise."

So I told my lawyer and he said, "Yeah people are going to say that, but when it comes down to getting money, you

**115**

won't get anything."

So they showed up again the next Saturday and asked, "Did you make a decision?"

I replied, "Well, before I do anything I'd have to have some money upfront. And if I can't pull it together, I'd give you your money back. But at least it shows that you're really serious." They wrote me out a check right there and handed it to me.

So I called my lawyer and said I got a check. Muscatine was the first one and then Minot was the second one. Third one was Dubuque, next one was in Clinton, and it moved pretty fast in the highway area at that time.

I remember going to my bookkeeper after we had been open for 12 months and asking, "How are we doing?"

She said, "You won't believe it, I got all the bills paid and you've got $350 in the bank."

I replied, "Does that cover giving a couple bucks to me too?" And she said, "That's paying you a salary too." And I said, "Whoa! It might work Joe."

Then about 6 months later, I went to talk to her again and said, "How are we doing?" She said, "Well, you'll be surprised."

"What do you mean?"

She said, "Everything's paid." And then she told me that I had $30,000 in the bank. It just kept moving like that. So that just kept me going.

------------------------

We created the taco pizza back in 1982 I think, or maybe it was '81. Some franchises we called wanted to put tacos in their restaurant. I said no, "I'll come up with something that's just as good as tacos."

After hanging up the phone and I said, "Oh my god! Now I've got to come up with something." So I sat around for a day or so and decided to try to make a taco pizza. I ended up getting it done and showed everybody in the office. And they said, "Oh my god! That's great, don't touch it anymore. Because," they said, "you're always trying to make things better. Just leave the taco pizza alone. It's great!" So that's how I came up with that.

------------------------

### *Advice on Starting a Business:*

Number 1, when you go to the bank, the best thing you can tell the bankers is, "I'm not going to take any salary until this thing gets flying."

They like to hear that. So I said, 'I'm not going to draw a salary out of it, at least for a couple months to make sure it's doing okay."

They liked that part.

Don't let friends and relatives discourage you. If you're going to listen to them, you're probably not going to do it. Everybody wants everything to be 100% sure that it's going to work. And I don't know anything out there that has a

100% chance of working.

I had so much negative, even my family, my brothers — *you're doing what?* Then after it takes off, my family in North Dakota says, 'I don't believe what's going on. He's got 4 stores now? We're flying down. We're going to see what he's doing."

They couldn't believe what was happening. So, it was a story come true.

The problem is people think, W*ell it just happened. You were just lucky.* I was putting in effort; my wife and I and kids all put in, we worked for it. So it's not something that just came easy.

**For a complete DVD of the full interview visit:**

**www.ceosecretsdvds.com/secret/book.html**

# Bonus CEO Interview Excerpt:

## *JOE SLAVENS*

*President & CEO of Northwest Bank & Trust Northwest Bank and Trust company is a $200million community bank located solely in the Quad Cities with 3 locations today.*

### *On Using Your Gut in Decisions:*

Sometimes it comes down to trusting your gut. Sometimes the numbers all add up, but it just doesn't seem to make sense. It's probably a great lesson to (over time) manage your gut, as well as manage your data. And when they align, it's wonderful. I think this is what small business owners do well. They trust their guts and do something different along the way.

### *On Sales and Marketing:*

I think that if you go back 30 years ago and more, the joke was that sales and marketing was being available to be approached on bended knee to approve every request for a loan. That's certainly been turned on its head, particularly here in the Quad Cities. We are, by one measure, the 8th most competitive banking market in the country. That's out of about 350 that they measure. Most people would think of Chicago or Los Angeles, but we have a very dispersed, very competitive banking market here.

So at the end of the day, sales and marketing is really the

life blood of the organization. We have to be able to present ourselves to potential followers, depositors, and investment management group customers that manage their money. We have to get in front of them. We have to stand out in the field. And naturally, we're going to do that differently with each client that we have. At the end of the day, if we have no sales and marketing activity, there is no bank.

### *3 Factors in Deciding to Start a Business:*

Number 1, is it something that you're interested in. Again, the old saying, is to find something you're passionate about and you'll never work a day in your life. That's an exaggeration, but I think we all need to find things that stimulate us and are interesting to us.

The second is a realistic check-in on what are our abilities. I might be really interested in a certain area, but if I look at the people that are in that business field and I don't have their skills sets, then it would not be a good area for me to open a business in.

The third is being able to sit down and basically have an understanding of what the financial model is. Where are we trying to end up? Who are the customers? Do I have to have a lot of very small customers? Am I going to have a few large customers? Am I comfortable that I'm going to be able to land those? Do I understand my expenses associated with being into this business?

### *How to Get Unstuck in a Current Business:*

I think it's important to step back and answer the questions:

*What do I think I have to do differently to move ahead?*

*Do I need to change the revenue stream or the expense stream?*

I have another philosophy and it is that we're all lazy. We like to get as much return for as little effort as humanly possible. And there's nothing wrong with that. That's what drives productivity and efficiency in America and around the world.

So asking the question, what are the three or four things that, if I change them, would move the needle at the end of the day? Follow that up with, what's my barrier to doing that? Is it because I've got all these little things that I'm doing so I'll just stop doing them? Is it because I need to hire someone to do the little things so I can do the big things? What are the barriers? Am I willing to do that? Is it money, is it time, is it changing my day? Then you must stand firm: I'm going to do it. You've got to understand it first.

Don't be afraid to fail. I think the only person who should be embarrassed of failure is the one who didn't put everything they had.

At the end of the day, there have been a lot of great businesses that have been developed because somebody tried. There have been a lot of great businesses that weren't because nobody said, *I'm willing to take the risk of failure.* You're going to have a plan and you sit down and say, *here's the shot I'm trying take it and trying to accomplish.* Bounce it off some people until it makes sense and you give it your all. Again, I think people will find a way to be successful. It's the nature of the beast. I would encourage people to be entrepreneurial – to take their shot and give it their all. In the end, something good will come of it.

**For a complete DVD of the full interview visit:**

**www.ceosecretsdvds.com/secret/book.html**

# Bonus CEO Interview Excerpt:

## *JIM RUSSELL*

*President & CEO of Russell Construction Commercial and Industrial design and construction. Over $100 million in annual revenue. Over one billion in sales in the last ten years.*

I started this business in 1983, when we were in a horrible recession and double digit unemployment and inflation. The very idea of going into the construction business was ludicrous. There really were more profitable businesses I could have gone into, like computers, but I didn't. I went into what I was passionate about and it was more about this sense of achievement than it was chasing the dollar.

Our philosophy is it's not about the money, it's about the achievement. It's about the competition, the adventure of starting and building something. That's probably why I ended up in the building business. It's very tangible and taking something from nothing to something is very rewarding.

The goal in the 1st year of business was to be credible and sustainable. And the big hairy audacious goal was to get the business to $5M in top line revenue by the 5th year. That was my hell or high water, I'm going to do that kind of goal. And that was all that mattered.

It's always been a grow, stabilize, grow, stabilize, grow, stabilize kind of model for 30 years. And we're now in another one of those growth modes where we're adding people, investing capital, stretching some boundaries and taking some entrepreneurial paths that are going to take us to another level.

### *On Figuring Things Out As You Go:*

In high school, when my friend and I started this home improvement business after graduating from high school, we secured a job re-roofing a house. It was a 2-story house. Neither one of us had done it before, and so we said, yes, figured out what we thought it should cost, got hired to do it and then literally went up on the roof with a book of how to shingle a roof and learned on the job.

So, there's a lot of yes, we can do it and let's figure it out as we go. Because one of the really fun things about what we do, whether it's a Skybridge in Davenport or a Figge Art Museum, using people who have never worked together before and predicting what it will cost before we start. I mean, in basic business philosophies that's pretty ludicrous.

But it works and feeds the entrepreneurial and problem-solving aspect and the attention-deficit of always wanting to do something different. But that's the business we're in. Our job is to say yes and then figure out how to do it.

Business is really simple. Whether it's yours or mine, it's get work, do work, keep score. That's what business is about.

So when you're growing a company, it's often get work, do work, keep score. You've got to keep pushing those three. If one gets too far ahead of the other, if you're selling more work than you can execute, well you're going to implode. Clients are going to be unhappy, obviously. If you build your execution up so that you've got more capacity than you have sales, you've got an overhead problem and you're going to fail on profitability there.

And the last one of keeping score is all about financial controls. When I started the business, the first 5 years were all about getting work. That was the focus. Doing work and keeping score didn't matter. Well, I had challenges with those. So the next 5 years, we had some beefing up of those 2 areas.

But from an entrepreneurial start-up business perspective, it's all about getting work. All else is moot. Who cares how big your CFO is if there's no dollars to count. Or if execution is great, but you don't have anything to execute on, it doesn't matter.

So from an entrepreneurial start-up perspective, it's figuring out to get work, how to create relationships and sell work and make opportunities happen. And that's a very sales, external relationship kind of process. It's a challenge.

For a complete DVD of the full interview visit:

**www.ceosecretsdvds.com/secret/book.html**

# Business Resource Directory

Due to the constantly changing nature of businesses, we have decided to post our business resource directory online for you.

You can download a free copy at www.profit911.biz/resources/directory.html

As of the time of this book publishing our resource directory includes:

*Answering Services*

*Suggested Reading List for Entrepreneurs*

*Merchant Account Processors*

*Outsourcing Websites*

*Printing Companies*

*Telephone & Tracking Phone Companies*

*Email Autoresponders*

*Marketing Automation*

*& Much More added every day*

# TWO FREE PASSES TO PROFIT 911 BUSINESS ACCELERATION BOOTCAMP

### A $1,994 VALUE

Justin Miller invites you and your spouse or business partner to attend his Profit 911 Business Acceleration Bootcamp as complimentary guests.

To register and for more information, go to:

**www.profit911.biz/seminar.html**

**IMPORTANT!** This one-time only offer is available to all purchasers of this book, Profit 911. Registration is subject to availability and space and/or changes to program schedule. The seminar must be attended within one year of purchasing this book. The value of admission is $997 per person. You are responsible for your own transportation, lodging, etc. but under no other financial obligation. We reserve the right to refuse admission to anyone we believe may hinder the seminar and to remove from the premises anyone we believe to be disrupting the seminar. We want this to be a pleasant learning experience for all involved.

www.ingramcontent.com/pod-product-compliance
Lightning Source LLC
Chambersburg PA
CBHW051318170526
45166CB00002B/597